What
I Tell
My
Heart

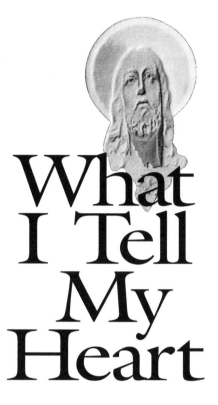

What I Tell My Heart

Prayers to a God
Whose Compassion Never Ends

Karen Ebert

PROVIDENCE HOUSE PUBLISHERS
Franklin, Tennessee

Printed in the United States of America

02   01   00   99   98   1   2   3   4   5

Library of Congress Catalog Card Number: 98-65875

ISBN: 1–57736–095–8

Cover design by Gary Bozeman

Cover art courtesy Paul Johnson

"Dear Lord and Father of Mankind" by John Greenleaf Whittier, page 28, from *United Methodist Hymnal,* United Methodist Publishing House, Nashville, Tennessee.

PROVIDENCE HOUSE PUBLISHERS
238 Seaboard Lane • Franklin, Tennessee 37067
800-321-5692

To my mother
BEVERLY BAUER
with thanks for teaching me
the power of God
and the power of words.

Contents

Foreword

HE WAS PRAYING IN A CERTAIN PLACE, AND AFTER HE HAD finished, one of his disciples said to him, "Lord, teach us to pray." (Luke 11:1)

Nearly everyone I encounter in the church these days expresses a longing to deepen their relationship with God. Many are wanting to find ways in which their daily lives can be experienced with God, shared with God, lived in God's gracious love. This book of prayers will assist anyone who uses them in their desire to live with God.

In his book, *Devotional Life in the Wesleyan Tradition,* Steve Harper reminds us that for John Wesley

> the chief instituted means of grace was prayer. It is not exaggerating to say that he lived to pray and prayed to live. He called prayer "the grand means of drawing near to God." Prayer had this importance because Wesley understood the Christian faith as a life lived in relationship with God through Jesus Christ. Because this is so, prayer was the key to maintaining that relationship. Furthermore, the absence of prayer was seen by Wesley to be the most common cause of spiritual dryness. *Nothing* (emphasis mine) could substitute for prayer in maintaining the spiritual life.

John Wesley sought to model his life after Jesus. The Bible stories tell us over and over again of the importance Jesus placed upon prayer. Wesley determined to make prayer a central part of each day. He encouraged his followers to engage regularly in public, family, and private prayer. "If you habitually neglect these, how can you expect that the light of God's countenance should continue to shine upon you?" Wesley wondered.

Karen Ebert's prayers help us to focus on God and assist us in bringing all of life to the very One who gives life. They remind and assure us of the God who is both Creator of the universe and friend of each of us. They invite us to listen for God's word as it beckons, reassures, and challenges us.

May these prayers help all who use them to engage in a more disciplined life of prayer and a more intimate life with God.

Sharon Zimmerman Rader, Bishop
Wisconsin Conference, United Methodist Church

About the Book

THE PRAYERS WITHIN THIS COLLECTION HAVE TOUCHED the hearts of the people of First United Methodist Church for the past four years in which Pastor Karen Ebert has served as our associate pastor. Each Sunday, Karen faithfully and sensitively leads the congregation to the throne of grace in her pastoral prayers.

In her words, she expresses beautifully the richness of God's grace which brings comfort and hope to the congregation.

In her words, she often speaks to the dark side of our humanity and challenges us to rise above.

In her words, she carefully says what many are feeling within.

These pastoral prayers are prayers shared in a liturgical setting on behalf of a congregation. Although they are Karen's prayers, when spoken in that hour of worship, they become our prayers and as such, touch the heart of God.

Rev. G. Keith Shroerlucke, Senior Pastor
First United Methodist Church, Green Bay, Wisconsin

What I Tell My Heart

This is what I shall tell my heart, and so recover hope: the favors of Yahweh are not all past, his kindnesses are not exhausted; every morning they are renewed.

—Lamentations 3:21–22 (JERUSALEM BIBLE).

Advent and Christmas

The Season of Promise

We turn to God now, to lift up together,
what each of us longs for alone,
and what all of us long for as one.

Blessed are you, Lord God of Israel.
    You have done great things for us,
        and have promised even greater.
    May our hearts be glad.

In this season of responsibilities by the list
    of shopping and decorating and baking and mailing,
we can be overcome by the hassles and bother and chaos.

So God, in the season of wonder lost in details,
    we pray that you will call to us again,
    grab our attention,
    and lift our eyes to the quiet skies
    to listen again for the words of angels.

How hard it is to believe the messages they bring:
    that our prayers, however crazy, might be answered;
    that promises, however old, are not forgotten;
    that your love, no matter how we've tested it,
        still holds fast;
    that no matter how mundane or vicious
        our world might become,
        you still yearn to enter it, and dwell among us.

Like Zechariah, we have our doubts. We have our doubts.
But if it were really true—
    if these things are really true . . .
        the possibility leaves us . . . speechless.

If it is true that you hear our wildest prayers,
    then maybe there is hope
    that the illness that eats our bodies might find healing;

that our children will grow up in a world without fear;
that peace may come even to the former Yugoslavia;
that plenty may fill even the cores of our biggest cities.

If it is true that your love for us, though strained, is not broken by our sin,
then perhaps we can find hope
that even if we have strayed
from a life of a disciplined spirit,
you have followed, and remain close enough to touch;
that despite the heinousness of the crimes we commit
against each other,
we may find a way to forgive each other,
and build again.

If it is true that your promises of prophets long ago are not forgotten,
then perhaps, just perhaps,
we may yet find that the presence of Christ
has come to transform our world *this* Christmas,
we may yet discover Christ, in some least expected place.

If it is true . . . we have hope.
May it be true, God.
It is for these things we find hard to believe, that we pray,
each time we join our voices in praying as Jesus taught us,
saying, "Our Father, who art in heaven. . . ."

How Long, God?

I am still caught up in our first hymn: "In the Bleak Midwinter."
It's the line, "frosty wind made moan" that has my attention.
The wind this fall has already become frosty—downright rude at times.
And the hardest part about it, is that I know this is only the beginning.
> *It will get a lot colder before it gets warmer.*
I could handle winter better if there was just the snow.
> *But the wind, pushing and pushing and pushing—*
> *that's what wears me thin.*
It is a season of bleakness out there, and frosty wind.
> *And sometimes it is such a season in here too.*
Are there winds, forces that push and push and push at you,
> *with no let-up in sight?*

Then in our silence, let them moan before God.

[silence]

God of all seasons, the chill has set in.
We brace ourselves against it and try to shake it off,
> but it still catches hold of us.
All that keeps us going is the knowledge that April will come again.

But unlike the months that we can count off on our fingers,
> waiting for the wind to break,
we have no way of marking how long
> until some other forces in our life will let go—if they ever will.

Cancer—How long until remission?
> How long will the remission last?
> Illness pushes and pushes.

Tensions in the family—Will the fighting someday cease?
> Or will the yelling someday cause us to crumble?
> Anger pushes and pushes.

Poverty—Is a job to be found soon?
>   Or will the savings be withered before that day?
>   Need pushes and pushes.

War—The fighting relents in one country, only to flare up in another.
>   Will the people ever have a chance to recover?
>   Violence pushes and pushes.

These forces, and more, swirl and taunt, and push.
We have braced ourselves against them.
We have tried to shake them off.
But our shouts are thrown back in our faces,
>   and our hands are useless in pushing back.
Some forces seem stronger than can be borne.

How long God?
We turn to you, the Maker of All Winds that Blow,
>   the One Whose Strength is Greater than All,
>   and we ask
How long do we have to wait?

This is what we tell our hearts and so renew our hope.
>   A God who can tilt the earth
>   to catch the warming rays of the sun
>   and turn the winter into spring
Can surely shift the balance
>   to keep us from blowing away.

Spring will come. We can hear its drip.
The pressures will ease.
I don't know how, I don't know when
>   Gracious God.
But we trust you.
And even in our bleakness, we have hope.

We join now, as a people of hope, praying the prayer of the followers of Christ:
>   "Our Father, who art in heaven. . . ."

Waiting in Confidence

God, we wait,
 and wait,
  and wait.
But though we are sometimes discouraged,
 we do not despair.

We see those in our family, and in this family of faith
 eaten by disease—nibbled away or swallowed whole—
 and we wait for the reign of Christ the healer
 to be complete in our world.
Come soon, Christ, and relieve the suffering of those we love.

We pick up index cards in the narthex,
 from a stack far too thick,
 cards that put a family into our care for Christmas.
As we try to meet the needs of those who lack
 food and diapers and mittens,
 we wait for the reign of Christ our Joy
 to be complete in our world.
Come soon, Christ, and relieve the gnawing emptiness
 of those we don't even know.

We read the daily news with breath held,
 and listen for the echoes of gunfire to fade,
 and for silence to fall over the ruins of Sarajevo,
  and the graves of all Bosnia.
And we wait for the reign of the Prince of Peace
 to be complete in our world.
Come soon, Christ, and end the violence of your children toward each other.

We wait and we hope,
 even though the record of the past
 and the evidence of the present
are tottering things on which to base a hope for the future.

But our hope is not built on these.

It is not in treaties and troops we trust.
It is not in food boxes and welfare we trust.
It is not in doctors and chemotherapy we trust.
It is in *you* we trust, God.

And if not in these ways,
then in another way, you *will* triumph.
And so our confidence rests in your loving care.
And when we can rejoice in the midst of misery,
and hope in the face of discouragement,
and work in the aftermath of failure,
we will know that your reign, Emmanuel, God With Us,
is complete in our lives.

In sure and certain hope of that day,
we pray together as we were taught, saying,
"Our Father, who art in heaven. . . ."

With Joseph

Surely you, like Joseph, have had the experience
   of having your best laid plans
      fall apart.
Sometimes, as for Joseph, these make for a life-changing moment.
Sometimes, they are minor aggravations.
Will you pause with me now,
      and listen, like Joseph, for the voices of angels,
      as God tries to guide you
         through the turns your life may be taking now.
Let us pray.

[silence]

Startling God,
      We can understand the fear that Joseph felt
      when he found out his fiancée was pregnant,
      and he was not the father.

He was afraid—things were not going as planned!
      His life was falling apart!
Many lives in this room, too, have taken turns for the worse,
      and we know the fear.

He was betrayed—
      The one he loved most seemed to have found another.
      And her words seemed so crazy, he took them for lies.
Many in this room, too, have known the searing pain
      of love turned inside out.
      And we know the fear.

He was humiliated—
      What would the people he lived with,
         worked with,
            worshiped with,
         think?
      How could he face them?

Many in this room, too have been shamed
  by what happens in our own lives.
  And we know the fear.

Mostly, he didn't understand.
  Why would Mary do this?
  What was she saying?
  Why would you, God, let this happen?
Many in this room, too,
  have anguished over the impenetrable ways you work,
  Upsetting God.
  And we know the fear.

But you sent an angel to Joseph, who said, "Fear not!"
And we know you send the same message
  to us in this room, too.
We know the fear to which the angel spoke.
Help us understand the trust
  that Joseph found in the angel's words.

Pour on *our* hearts the cooling trust,
  that washes fear away,
And allows us
  to embrace
   what and who the world tells us to reject;
  to celebrate
   what the world would hide;
  to go calmly ahead
   with plans the world would balk at;
Send us trust in you this day,
and help us past our fear,
  so we can thank you for the unexpected opportunities
  that you hide
  in our life's calamities.

We join our hearts and voices in praying
  the prayer which Christ taught
  to all who fear and to all who trust:

"Our Father, who art in heaven. . . ."

A Sixty-Second Space

Christmas preparations have now reached a fevered pitch.
  If we go any faster,
  or try to do any more,
  we may just fly apart in a million little pieces.
But God didn't come at Christmas to give us the gift of a nervous breakdown.
This is not what God wants from us.
God just wants us to open up a little space to let Christ in.

Here's a little space—about sixty seconds wide.
Take it, and use it to forgive yourself for not creating the perfect, magazine Christmas.
Because God has already forgiven.

In silence, let us pray.

[silence]

Hello God.
We know you are out there, just on the edge of our lives.
    We're trying to help you make a grand entrance,
    and we have only five days left to do it in.
God, we are getting tired of the holiday and it has not even arrived.
    We'd just like to get it over with.
    If you're coming, God, please hurry.
God, the news depresses us.
    All those skeletal children in Somalia.
    All those bombs in Bosnia.
    All those jobless, lined up under the Christmas lights.
Prince of Peace, we need you. Please hurry.

God, our lives are a little scary.
    The ones we hold dear are snatched away by cancer, and car accidents.
    Children are born imperfect.
    Holidays neither ease our pain, nor calm the secret fears that hound us.
Mighty Counselor, where are you? Please hurry.

God, sometimes we think we catch glimpses of you,
    in a blazing angel on the lawn, next to the electrified Santa Claus;
    In the pure unadulterated hope in children's eyes;
    In unexpected generosities.
Lord of light, slow us down, or we'll miss you.

God, it took at least seven days to make the world.
But our expectations for a single twenty-four hour period in December
    make creation a slow-motion event.
    God, it was only in the unhurried hours of the middle of the night
        that you opened a crack into eternity.
Slow us down, Emmanuel,
    that we might reach through that crack and touch the Christ.

Thank you, God.
We'll take a slow deep breath now,
and pray together the timeless words of prayer,
    taught us by the Christ of Christmas . . .
"Our Father, who art in heaven. . . ."

Christmas Eve

In the dark of the night,
    in the cold of winter,
        some shepherds went about their usual business
        watching the sheep, keeping them safe.
They did not know that they were about to be surprised
    by the flutter of wings
    the blinding of light
    the otherworldly voices of angels,
    and by the goodness of God.

In the dark of the night,
    in the cold of this winter,
        we pause now from our usual business,
        to keep a silent vigil.
We hope for the surprises of God.
We long for the surprises of God.
We wait now for God's goodness,
    in the silence of prayer.

[silence]

As we listen for the angels, God, hear *our* prayers. Amen.

Epiphany

Wash Me Clean

Some Sundays, about noon, I look at my hands. And though they look perfectly normal, I feel as if I have shaken hands with every germ in the city, and I long to run soapy water over them, before I go home to eat my lunch.

Some days, when people look at us, they see that everything looks perfectly normal. But inside, we feel a film of grime that the world has left on us. Or we feel the stain caused by some unspoken act we've committed. And we long to be washed clean of it, before we can go on with our lives.

This morning, as we sit in silence, look within yourselves, and seek out those corners which need a good scrubbing. Remember that even when the outside looks perfectly normal, God can see within, and God can make the foulest clean.

In silence, we pray.

[silence]

God of all, and God of each,
> this morning we look back to that early washing of us in our baptism;
we think how as small drops of water trickled over our heads,
>> we were swept up into the great river of all who follow Christ,
>> of all who have ever, will ever follow Christ.
And we give thanks.
> We give thanks that we are part of the rush of the waters,
> that we are carried along in its flow,
> that we are borne up on its power.

God of all, and God of each,
> wash over us again this morning, and create in us a clean heart.
Rinse away the sins, the fears, the worries that weigh us down,
> and lift us again into the flow of the followers of Christ.

We ask for cleansing as well for those we can name,
> whose hearts are clouded and dulled by many burdens—
> by illness; by abuse;
> by the pressures of their jobs; by the stresses of school;
> by decisions waiting to be made, and by decisions out of their hands;
create in them clean hearts.

God of all and God of each,
   we know how, out of the great flood of petitions which go up to you,
you still listen to each of our prayers,
   dropped into the silence.
Hear our prayers.
   And wash us. Wash away our guilt and our despair,
      let us soak in your love until we are wrinkled and pruny,
   until our sin and sorrow are floated away on a sea of forgiveness.
   Until with towel rubbed vigor, we can step out into the day,
      refreshed,
   and see the world anew, and clean.

God of all, and God of each, create in us clean hearts.
We pray in the name, and in the way of the one who taught us to say:
"Our Father, who art in heaven. . . ."

Show Us Faces

God of colorful palette, God of broken chains,
    as we sit in the kaleidoscopic glow of the stained glass,
    we are aware of the sameness of most of the faces which surround us.
We note this as a confession,
    not that we have consciously turned away
    from those who are different from us.
But it is evidence that we have not made strong enough
    our efforts to turn towards those,
    whose skin, and accent, and income,
    do not match our own.

Bring to our minds this moment,
    images of those who are not like us,
    but who are, like us, made in your image.
Show us the faces of immigrants,
    and refugees,
        from decades past and days recent.
Show us the faces of those whose ancestors
    lived here long before ours—
    part of the land itself,
    or brought here as captives.

Show us the faces of those who worship you this very hour,
    halfway around the world,
    or half a mile from here,
    using words we do not understand,
        but you do,
        and are praised and thanked.
Show us the faces of those who live just doors away,
    who have never entered these doors,
    or felt your love,
    because we have never invited them.
Show us the faces in all their diverse glory,
    this morning, and in the days ahead,
    and draw us to the beauty
    you have painted in their eyes,

as surely as you have painted it in ours,
for we are all your children,
and we carry your image.

God of colorful palette, God of broken chain,
free those kept prisoner by the invisible walls of prejudice,
including us.
Free us to open our doors, as well as our hearts,
to invite our brothers and sisters in.

We pray this in the name of Jesus,
whose skin was probably much darker than my own,
but loves us all no matter our color,
and taught us all to pray together,
"Our Father, who art in heaven. . . ."

Remembering

Some days, I am absentminded.
A lot of days, I am absentminded.
Do you have days like that?
> *When you forget the kids at practice?*
> *When you forget your best friend's birthday?*
> *When you walk by someone who has suffered a great loss,*
> > *and forget to offer a word of comfort?*
I am glad that God does not forget.

In this time of silence, perhaps it would help you in your prayers,
> *to dig back into your buried memories,*
> *and offer up to God the people you have lost track of;*
> *the causes you once supported,*
> > *but abandoned somewhere along the line;*
> *the experiences you never resolved, and so you just set them aside.*
In silence, we now meet the God of memory.

[silence]

O God who remembers all that we forget,
remember for us, all the people we have lost:
> grade school teachers;
> college roommates whose Christmas cards come back
> > marked "Address Unknown";
> neighbors from the town before this one.
Remember them, and keep them safe.
May our prayers for them reach you, and may you reach them.
Remember, O God, even when we forget.

Remember for us the issues that once made us blaze with passion,
> but have now cooled to dust and ashes in us:
> keep working for peace in El Salvador;
> feed the children in Ethiopia;
> disarm both our weapons and our prejudices
> > towards the countries that once made up the Soviet Union.
Our attention spans are short, God.

Continue the work you started, even when we, like small children,
    have wandered away to new attractions.
Remember, O God, even when we forget.

Remember with us, God, the anniversaries of deaths, and of losses—
    both ours, and those of the people we know:
    soothe the pain rekindled by the calendar,
        which reminds us that a husband has been gone for a decade;
        that this would have been a child's birthday;
        that last year at this time, we had hopes that now seem foolish.
Remember, O God, when no one else does.

Remember with us, the small acts of heroism we have done.
Recall our good intentions, and our fervent desire to please you.
We have, each of us, dedicated our lives to you,
    at some moment or another.
When our actions betray our commitment,
    and our love for you is hidden,
        remember, O God.
Remember, even when no one else does.

Remember, O God, what we ourselves are afraid to remember.
Remember the wrongs done to us,
    the abuses of body and spirit, which, though we may push them down,
    continue to surface—to our harm, and the harm of those around us.
Remember, O God, until justice is served,
    until healing is found,
        and until forgiveness is possible.
Remember, O God, even when we ourselves cannot.

Remember, in days to come, God,
        when age has robbed us of coherent speech
            and control of our bodily functions,
        remember the people we once were.
            The talents of our youth,
            the accomplishments of our maturity,
            and the dignity of our aging are within us,
                even when the flesh fails.

Remember who we really are God,
even when we ourselves no longer can.

O God of all memory, we now pray together the prayer
which binds us together with all who follow Christ,
even those beyond our memory:
"Our Father, who art in heaven. . . ."

Listening

Let us enter into our time of prayer by singing the last three verses of "Dear Lord and Father of Mankind."

> *O Sabbath rest by Galilee, O calm of hills above,*
> *where Jesus knelt to share with thee the silence of eternity,*
> *interpreted by love.*

> *Drop thy still dews of quietness, till all our strivings cease;*
> *take from our souls the strain and stress, and let our ordered lives*
> *confess*
> *the beauty of thy peace.*

> *Breathe through the heat of our desire thy coolness and thy balm;*
> *let sense be dumb, let flesh retire; speak through the earthquake,*
> *wind, and fire,*
> *O still, small voice of calm.*

[silence]

God, we sing to you today,
    to help us pray, to help us say what we cannot find words for.
But we also sing,
    to help us listen.
When our tongues must shape another's words,
    our own are held in check,
    and we listen to the conversation
    that has taken place between you and the one who wrote the song.

Help us listen today, God,
    for what you are saying to others,
        but have not said to us,
    and to listen to what you may be saying to us through others.

Help us to listen to those who contradict us,
    who don't listen to us,
    or who argue us down;

or who could not possibly care less
about things we care for most.
Help us hear in these people
echoes of how we sound to others;
and perspectives on our priorities.
Speak to us, God, through those we would rather not hear.

Help us to listen to those we overlook and ignore.
To the children, too young, we think, to make sense.
To the aged, who are, we think, out of touch.
To those who bore us,
To those we find unintelligent or naive,
and to those we have simply never noticed.
Help us to hear in these people
surprises of unexpected grace,
a call to humble ourselves,
and gentle reminders that no one is overlooked,
by the one that matters most.
Speak to us, God, through those we have tuned out.

We know that you are not silent, God.
But sometimes we forget that you may not always be talking to us.
Teach us to be alert for your whispered words,
so that even when we are not paying the slightest attention to you,
we may overhear your love-talk with the world,
and know that it is meant for us as well.

And now we put our tongues to work again, to shape another's words,
as we pray using the words taught to us and to our parents,
and listen for what you have said to the world through their prayers.
"Our Father, who art in heaven. . . ."

God of Ages

If you ask children, they will tell you how they see God,
*   often old, sometimes bearded, usually in the clouds.*
Maybe when you were that age, you saw God the same way—
*   or maybe differently.*
Probably, your mental picture of God has changed some over the years,
*   as you have met God in different places and in different ways.*
*   God has a way of coming to us in ways that meet our needs.*

In our silent prayers this morning,
*   I invite you to close the lids of your eyes,*
*   and open the eyes of your mind,*
*   and to see how God appears to you—*
*   however comfortingly familiar, or startlingly upsetting that might be.*
In our silent prayers, close your eyes and let God be God,
*   let God be God for you.*

[silence]

God of all ages, as our own years change how we see you,
    we ask you now to change the way we see our time in life.

God of youth, we pray today for the children.
We pray for the difficulties of being young—
    for the frustration of being powerless and dependent.
    For the hard work of learning, when everything is new.
    For the bodies that cannot yet do all they want them to.
    For the struggle to sort out their own identities,
        unique from parents.
    For the fears of what the future will bring,
        and the decisions it will require.
    For the difficulty of coping with this fast-moving,
        complicated, frightening world.

God of the young,
we pray that you will help those now young to see the gifts of their youth:
    the excitement of discovery,
    the hope of an entire lifetime yet ahead of them,

the sure and certain care of parents they can count on,
the wonders they will know, and create,
that those before them never saw.
God be with the young.

God of those in the middle of life,
we pray for the difficulties of those years.
For the heavy weight of responsibility,
for work and job,
for growing children
and aging parents.
For the sudden knowledge that half of life has passed,
and concerns about decisions made long ago.
For the exhaustion of too much to do,
too many debts,
too many options.

God of the in-between times,
help those now in the middle to know the blessings of this time:
The opportunity to make a difference in the world.
The chance to see their children become adults.
The satisfaction of work well done,
and well-developed skills appreciated.
Health and independence and ability.
God be with those in middle age.

God of the aging,
we pray for those who have lived long lives, and face the trials of being old:
For bodies which seem to decay day by day.
For memories which slip and fade.
For too much free time, and a sense of uselessness.
For loneliness.
For dependence, returning again.

God of many years,
give a vision of the beauty of age to those who see only burdens:
Families grown and expanding, who care deeply about them.
The mature love of husband and wife.
The freedom of retirement.
A wealth of memories from many years.

The wisdom accumulated from experience, good and bad.
A sense of accomplishment.
The certainty that you are with them, even beyond this life.

God be with those who are aged.

God, whatever the age we are in, be with us, and help us to be with each other.
We pray together now, the prayer of the church in all ages,
　　as Jesus taught us to pray: "Our Father, who art in heaven. . . ."

We Lift Up Our Hearts

It's Valentine's day.
You're probably about romanced to pieces—
hearts everywhere you look—
hearts of lace,
hearts of candy,
hearts of construction paper;
stamped with tiny red words,
shot through with arrows,
filled with chocolate.

Is your heart full this morning?
Brimming with gratitude for the special someones in your life?
Or is your heart so empty it is collapsing on itself?
Either way, in our silent time this morning, open your heart to God in prayer.

[silence]

O thou Great Lover of our Souls,
even in the silence,
you hear the sounds of all we have caged up in our hearts,
of all that pours out when we open them to you.
We open our hearts, and out gush all the tears we have held in all week.
Each searing memory,
each tooth-grinding frustration,
each pain we see in someone we love but can do nothing to ease,
fills us up, drip by drip, until we can hold no more.
Let us cry on your shoulder, comforting God,
so that there is room in our hearts for joy.

We open our hearts and out rattle our fears, like long-hidden bones.
We hide them from the world, lest the world judge us,
ridicule us,
condemn us.
In our need to be strong, we hold our fears within and they grow like tumors.
Let your perfect love cast them out, accepting God,
so that there is room for peace.

We open our hearts, and out flutter our smiles,
>with the sound of a startled flock of pigeons.
They surprise even us with their unpredictable independence.
>We hadn't realized there were so many in there.
But the tingly delight of having our hand caressed by someone we love
>puts one in there,
>and so does the warmth of sincere praise,
>and the excitement of hearing good news.
They brood in there, until they swoop and dip and soar,
>and lift us off our feet.
Release them, God of Eagle's wings,
>so that there is room for even more.

We open our hearts,
>and out fall the obligations we carry with a mighty thud.
There is so much expected of us God.
Some are inconsequential—
>the dictates of fashion, the scattered errands and requests,
But some fill our hearts with concrete—
>the daily need to perform at work,
>the burden of caring for someone with a chronic illness.
They are inescapable,
>we are chained to them by love and guilt.
Cut them loose freeing God,
>so there is room . . . for you.

May our hearts be free of sin and sadness,
May our hearts be full of praise and gladness,
>as we continue to open them to you in prayer, as Jesus taught us, saying,
"Our Father, who art in heaven. . . ."

Lent

The Length of Days

Forty days is a long time.
When Jesus spent forty days in the wilderness,
>   *with little to eat or drink,*
>   *I'll bet those days got long.*
Hunger and thirst and too much sun
>   *can test the endurance of even a faithful man.*

Forty days is a long time.
Lent, the forty-day season, comes from the word lenchten, "to lengthen."
It refers to the lengthening of days in spring.
>   *But the days of Lent are long in other ways as well.*

There are days in our lives that are too long,
>   *and seasons which test our endurance.*
In our time of silence this morning,
>   *I invite you to lift to God those times which stretch your soul.*

[silence]

O God, end of our journey and source of our strength,
>   we turn to you in days that are long,
>   and we pray, not just for ourselves,
>   but for all people
who find they reach the end of their resources before the end of their days.

We pray for those whose days are long with waiting.
>   Those whom illness forces to wait in a hospital bed,
>   or to keep vigil beside one.
>   Those who wait for an answer
>   from a sister, a friend, an employer.
>   Those who wait for an end to war,
>   listening to the tentative silence in Sarajevo,
>   listening to gunfire in the night in our inner cities.
In the midst of days that are long, be swift God.

We pray for those whose days are long with toil.
Those who work in jobs that are stressful and demanding.
Those who work in jobs which break the back
without filling the soul.
Those whose work never ends, in caring for
the helpless infant
or the dependent aging parent.
In the midst of days that are long, give strength, God.

We pray for those whose days are long in yearning.
Those who hope for healing,
those who long for justice,
those who sigh for rest.
In the midst of the long days of Lent,
keep clear the promise of resurrection,
that at the end of our long days,
we may rejoice.

With the confidence of your children,
we join our voices to pray as Jesus taught: "Our Father, who art in
heaven. . . ."

Casting Out Fear

When Jesus looked out over his beloved Jerusalem, he lamented "How often have I desired to gather your children together as a hen gathers her brood under her wing, and you were not willing" (Luke 13:34).

God still longs to gather us close.
Let us turn toward God,
and admit to God what it is that keeps us
from running as fast as we can to the shelter of her wings.

[silence]

The Bible says:
"Love has been perfected among us in this:
    that we may have boldness on the day of judgement . . .
    There is no fear in love, but perfect love casts out fear."
You know how we need those words, God.
Because you know our fears.
    You know the wordless terrors that snatch our hearts,
    the monsters under our beds that we didn't outgrow,
    but which matured with us into adult-size anxiety.

You know the fears that keep us from trusting the world.
Too many nights as we lie awake,
    they creep from beneath the bed to whisper in our ears:
    Will the money make it to the end of the month,
        or will an unforeseen crisis push us over the edge?
    Will the children survive to adulthood,
        or will AIDS or alcohol, or God-knows-what take them down?
    Will there be anything left for us when we grow old,
        of social security, or personal security, or the earth?

God, you know the fears that keep us from trusting ourselves.
Too many days these monsters perch on our shoulders and nag,
    You really aren't very good at your job.
    You really don't deserve such an easy life.
    Why would anyone love you?

God, we could handle those fears, with you at our side.
We could stare them down by looking through the bold hope in your eyes—
Except for those fears which keep us from trusting . . . you.
Why should we risk ridicule for being a fanatic?
Is following Christ really worth the hard choices—
friendships compromised,
promotions turned down,
choosing between family and you?
Are we so certain you will be there for us
when we've let go of our culture's priorities?

God of open arms, we long to run to you,
We long to be gathered,
as much as you long to gather us up under your wings.
But we are paralyzed with fear,
we hide our heads,
hold our breath,
and dare not even move from where we are,
lest the monsters catch us and eat us whole.
O God, may we be rocked to sleep,
and gently crooned awake,
to the constant certainty of your love song:

Perfect love casts out all fear.
love casts out all fear.
love casts out fear.
love.

For your love that lets our breathing resume, we thank you God.
For your love that makes us bold to change, we thank you God.
For your love that calls us to your side
no matter how justified the fear—
we offer our undying praise.

Until we can display the confidence of children of God,
and live the prayer which Jesus taught,
we will teach each other by saying together,
"Our Father, who art in heaven. . . ."

Acts of God

They call them acts of God.
I don't suppose the insurance companies started the practice
of blaming God for all natural disasters,
but they sure have perpetuated it by making it a legal term.
Acts of God—as in earthquake, tornado, flood, hail, lightning.
Acts of God—as in things you try to protect yourself against.

Let me bring to mind a verse from scripture,
a passage that may be extremely familiar to you:
"God did not send his Son into the world to condemn the world,
but in order that the world might be saved through him."

I ask you to keep that in your mind as we begin a time of silent prayer.
Keep in mind God's hope for the world—
to save, not to destroy—
as you try to identify the acts of God that you have seen this last week.

[silence]

Our Light and Our Salvation,
Whom shall we fear?
Certainly not you.

Forgive us that though we may know those words from John's gospel by heart,
we have not taken them to heart.

Some days it's hard, God, to believe that you want to save us, not condemn us.
We feel as if you are a cosmic cop,
giving us rules just so we will break them,
lying in wait, just to catch us messing up,
sending us Christ, just to be a secret code word of faith.

It can be frustrating, and frightening,
to see the world as a trap,
and every act of yours as punishment.

God, we would ask you to have mercy, to relent,
to take away your condemnation.
Except . . .
if the scripture is right, the condemnation is not there to begin with.

And so gentle loving God,
we ask that you would help us feel your everlasting arms around us.
Help us hear your tender words of comfort and encouragement.
Help us see in Christ the incredible gift of your coming among us,
beckoning to us, not threatening.

Hold us gently,
until we recognize the saving "acts of God,"
acts which are far more abundant in this world
than the fearsome "acts of God."
Lead us gently,
until we begin to participate in those saving acts,
through our gifts to those who suffer,
our kind words and deeds,
our healing and nurturing actions.
Speak to us gently,
Until our fear of you,
is turned into awe,
and with wide eyes,
we can turn to you with gratitude and joy,
and live in your world as a birthday party,
rather than a prison.

God who loves us,
in love we now join our voices in the way Jesus taught his disciples:
"Our Father, who art in heaven. . . ."

By Name

God of swirling galaxies,
Lord of the atoms of dandelions,
    we are lost in your presence.
It is hard not to feel overlooked
    in the vastness of your creation.
If our entire planet were to explode,
    it would cause not a ripple in the universe.
Why should you care—or notice—
    if one average person
    in one average town
    in the ordinary Midwest
    feels life is falling apart?

If our government has never heard of us,
    if the neighbors never ask,
    if our fellow Christians overlook us,
    and even our family does not notice there is a problem,
why would you, O God, care?
There are days, when we are convinced we are right, God.
We know you don't care, because we see no evidence of you.
    In the places we expect you
        we find only echoing silence, and empty cold,
        and vacant stares of non-recognition.

But somehow, most days, we know better.
We know that it is the most important thing in the world to you that:
    Eunice is sick and tired of hospitals.
    Mark is worried about the test results.
    Mollie felt abandoned when no one visited.
    O. B. is anxious for Ginny's recovery.
    Leah still aches for her mother.
And that in each of our anxious moments,
    we are the most important thing to you,
    and you are there with us,
    soothing us,
    and saying our names, over and over.

O Thank you, God. O Thank You.
For a love stronger than even parents have for us,
    for a caring so close it is within us,
    and for your concern for us
    that never seems a burden to you,
    just a natural expression
    of your passion for me,
and Keith, and Jim, and Sharon, and Anne, and Vi, and Brad,
    and all the rest of us.

As you have hallowed each of our names by carrying them in your heart,
    so now we bless your name, by praying together as Jesus taught,
    and saying, "Our Father, who art in heaven. . . ."

Upsetting Arrival

If we were given the choice between Barabbas and Jesus,
between the familiar evil
and the uncomfortable challenge we don't understand,
I wonder what we would choose?

When we are offered the choice—and we are—
to continue in our path, however unsatisfying,
or to take the risk of Christ, what do we choose?
In silence, let us pray for our choices, and their consequences.

[silence]

Christ who entered Jerusalem on a donkey, and riled up the crowd,
invade our lives this day, in ways we least expect,
and disturb the peace.

Upset those who think that power lies in control and force,
and that those who are strong must never dare look foolish.

Disturb those who think that the world is in human hands,
and that since it is we who hold the fate of ourselves and others,
it is only we who matter.

Stir up the hopes of these who think that nothing can change,
and that suffering and struggle will last always.

Startle us from our certainty that death holds the last word,
and from our cynicism at the endurance of your passionate love for us.

O God, the hoofbeats of Jesus' donkey sound like distant thunder to us,
the rumble of an approaching storm.

Our scalps prickle in anticipation.
For it is we who will be upset and disturbed,
as it is we who will be stirred and startled.

God of the humble donkey,
    of the defenseless accusation, of the friends' betrayal,
        of the humiliating death—
        you know too well the trials we face.

God of the empty tomb,
    of the shaken-off burial clothes,
        of the ecstatic women at dawn,
        may we know with you the new life of resurrection. Amen.

A Piercing Vision

It has become familiar to us,
    the picture of a body nailed to a cross.
But see again,
    the blood on the brow, and the wrist, and the ankle,
    leaving a glistening red track through the dust
    before becoming cracked and dusty itself.

The words have become smooth from use by years of tongues:
    crucifixion;
    a man despised and rejected . . . well-acquainted with grief
    "Why have you forsaken me?"
But listen again
    to the gasp of pain, and fear, and abandonment;
hear again,
    the bewilderment of those who put their faith in Jesus,
    only to have him arrested, ridiculed, and executed.

As we enter into silence, to face our God,
    listen and look again to the brutal facts of the death.
For it is against this despair and emptiness
    that the surprise of Easter will gain its
    startling, astonishing power.
In silence, let us pray.

[silence]

O God of suffering,
    If we have immunized ourselves to the suffering of Christ,
    is it any wonder we are hardened to the pain of the world,
    of these other daughters and sons of yours?
The sight of hunger-swollen bellies,
    of the eerie green tracer bullets in war-torn night skies,
    of the unshaven man making a bed of newspapers on a heating grate—
These sights are so common on our television screens
    that they no longer pierce us—though they pierce you.
Forgive us, that we do not see the pain you suffer with your children.

O God of Glory,
>
> If we can yawn and roll over on the day to remember resurrection,
>
> is it any wonder that we fail to notice the new life
>
> > offered to us every morning?

We are too accustomed to riches.
We are too used to the smooth and flawless,
> to the abundance that goes beyond need,
> to having our own way.

Too sated with miracles, we fail to perceive what you have given us.
We pause now to thank you for your lavish goodness, and your boundless love.

O God who speaks life in the face of death,
the signs of resurrection surround us,
> from the grass that grows through the asphalt,
> to the person who walks from the hospital, healed.

At least for one day, we will not take this for granted.
We rejoice that not even for one day do you take us for granted.

We pray now in the pattern of the
> one whose death and life we dare not forget, saying,
> "Our Father, who art in heaven. . . ."

Easter and Pentecost

Cloudy Easter Sunday

I read to you from a book called Magnificent Defeat *[Frederick Buechner]:*

> *I cannot tell you . . . what I think I would have seen if I had been there myself. . . .*
> *But I can tell you this: that what I believe happened and what in faith and great joy*
> *I proclaim to you is that he somehow GOT UP, with the life in him again, and the*
> *glory upon him. And I speak very plainly here, very unfancifully, even though I do not*
> *understand my own language. I was not there to see it any more than I was awake to*
> *see the sunrise this morning, but I affirm it as surely as I do that by God's grace the*
> *sun did rise this morning because that is why the world is flooded with light.*

Even if you did not see it rise,
> *even if you cannot see it out right now for the clouds,*
> *still the light is shining.*
In our lives as well, though we cannot always pinpoint the source,
> *we feel the radiance of God's presence.*
In this moment of silence, let us thank God for the light which
> *shines on us all.*

[silence]

God of resurrection, sometimes we miss you in the crowd,
> lose track of what you do, and its importance to us.
But not today.

Today, like no other, we understand what you offer us:
> a fresh start.
Though the grass has barely begun to gossip about green amidst the thatch,
> though tulips may be curling up their frostbitten fingers for warmth,
> though even the sun itself seems to be waiting behind a curtain of
> clouds for another day to make its grand earth-warming entrance,
we know that you are not to be held back.

If the constraints of history were not enough to hem you in the first century,
> then surely the twentieth century offers no greater challenge.

If the deaf ignorance of our apathy did not wear you down,
    surely there is no match for your persistence in pursuit of us.
If the barbed armor of our sin were not enough to keep you at bay,
    then surely nothing else we can do will keep you from us.
If even the cold weight of death could not pin you down,
    then there is no power in heaven or on earth
    that your love cannot endure, resist, and melt through.

This certain knowledge of the great power of your love
    runs through us like the sap rising.
Surely, there is no force that can imprison us,
    empowered by your great grace.
With you at our side, we always break free.
    Alleluia! Alleluia! Alleluia!
We pray in the name of the Risen One, saying together,
"Our Father, who art in heaven. . . ."

Proclaiming Resurrection

Easter God,
> we, your resurrection people
> have gathered not far from the wonder of the empty tomb,
>> to worship you
>> and shout the good news to the world.

But we admit,
> as you must already know
> that this week,
> we do not shout it very loudly,
> and our tongues stumble over Alleluias.

In Tokyo and Yokohama, the people cannot breathe for fear.
> The air is poisoned by those who want to harm.
Closer to home, we acknowledge that on the twenty-fifth Earth Day,
> our own air is still a threat to lung and climate,
> even when no one aims to hurt.
But muting our gospel proclamation most of all
> is the image of the crumbling remains
> of Oklahoma City's Federal Building.
The knowledge that someone could *choose*
> to loose such destruction,
> inflict such pain,
> and kill so many, in less time than it takes to flinch,
stuns us to silence.

How can we proclaim the resurrection in the face of *this*?

God, I know I am not the only one here
> whose tears have wet the newspapers,
> not the only one who has screamed prayers of rage to you.
Though the victims are strangers to us,
> we find ourselves easily in their places,
> and the weight of the rubble crushes our hearts too.

But God, in the face of this, we find
the *only* thing strong enough to resist
the agony, the despair,
the rage that seeks vengeance and slashes the innocent,
the only thing we can offer *is* the resurrection.

O Easter God,
to those who have died, we proclaim the resurrection.
Gather them into your arms,
and introduce them to the life that never ends.

O Easter God,
to those who have lost a husband, a wife, a friend, a child—
we proclaim the resurrection.
Bind their hearts with your love,
and assure them that even *this* death
cannot tear your love from them.

O Easter God,
to those who dig and search and heal,
we proclaim the resurrection.
Continue to send the power of your undefeatable care
through them.

O Easter God,
to those who planned and executed this horrific deed,
we proclaim the resurrection,
and count on you to find a way to return life for death,
and offer the mercy and forgiveness that we cannot.

We remember, O Easter God,
that it was for such people as all of these you came;
it was in such senseless pain you died;
and it was despite such evil that you arose;
So that in the face of *even this*,
we can proclaim the resurrection until our hearts are convinced.
We join now, our hearts and voices
in the name and the words of the Risen one, saying, "Our Father, who art
in heaven. . . ."

Spring in Wisconsin

My husband's sister called Tuesday from Maryland.
She's a California girl. She's never lived in Wisconsin.
So she was shocked to discover
that our temperatures are in the 50s to low 60s (on a good day),
and we are loving it.

We need to get her out here in April some year,
so she can learn what we know:
That spring is a rare delicacy to savor,
long in preparation, quick in passing,
and incomparable in its ability
to draw you back to the earth,
and the God who made it.
In our silent time of prayer,
I invite you to give thanks to God for spring
in Wisconsin.

[silence]

The lawn is wearing green velvet.
The maple tree is draped in a veil of red lace.
The sky is a shade of intense blue; we are not daring enough
        to paint our own ceilings.

The wind brushes the hair from our foreheads
        with a touch softer than a baby's fingers.
The sunshine has found strength enough
        to warmly massage our winter-tired backs.

The earth calls to us, and we long to be with it,
        to leave behind vinyl and concrete, and plaster,
        and to comb the debris from earth's hair,
        and to run on the soft shoulder of earth,
        and to throw ourselves into the inviting breath of it,
        and to smell the rich, dark smell of it,
        still cold between our fingers.

It is now that we know we are of the earth,
      made of its dust and humus,
      participant in its humming rhythms
      and its rolling cycles.
In your image, O God,
      and of your substance, O Earth,
      we are made.
God, Creator,
      you have blessed us with
      all plants heavy with seed,
      and all trees which drop fruit,
      and all creatures that run,
          or fly, or crawl, or breathe!

Make us a blessing
      to this earth of yours
      and all that are part of it
      so that we may never lose the blessings
      we receive from your hand,
in the kiss of spring.
In Earth's graciousness and abundance,
      in its diversity and cleverness,
      in its balance of give and take, birth and death,
      in its returning from death,
      in its beauty for beauty's sake,
we see your will, Creator God.

Keep us, who wield power beyond proportion,
      within the bounds of your will,
      so that your will may be *done,*
          on earth
      as in its model, heaven.

We pray now, with all your children of Earth, and sky,
saying, "Our Father, who art in heaven. . . ."

Silence Us

This is a Sunday to honor Native American people,
> *and some of the traditions which have come into our Christian faith*
> > *through them,*
> > *thereby enriching our faith.*
One practice which holds a large place in many native cultures, is silence.
To lead us into our silent prayers today,
> *I share with you this prayer, out of a native tradition:*
"Teach me, O great spirit of silence, to find thy presence on the altar of inward peace. In deep love and joy to vibrate with the eternal mystery of creation. To behold you in every life expression. To feel you there, in every beat of my heart. Through the depth of meditation, I receive thy supreme light—O thou glorious Spirit of Silence" (United Methodist Book of Worship).

In silence, let us pray.

[silence]

God,
Great Spirit,
Star Abiding One,
You who ride the winds and speak to us through the seas,
> you startle us with many voices.
We are so accustomed to seeking you out here,
> in our carpeted,
> > closed-in,
> > > choir-accompanied, house of worship,
> that we forget that we can find you anywhere else.
We do, in fact, sometimes *deny* that you can be found anywhere else.

We are harsh with those who do not see you as we do,
> do not praise you as we do,
> do not call you as we do.
We have, as a people,
> sometimes destroyed beliefs and practices,
> and even people, in defense of your name,
> for the advancement of your name.

Not so long ago, nor so far away.
Perhaps even here and now.

Forgive us, God, our zeal to protect you,
  which only locks you away from others . . . and ourselves.

Help us to hear you in ways we do not expect.
Help us to understand that you speak in many languages,
  and perhaps most often, without words.
Help us to find you,
  as did the people who walked this spot before our European ancestors,
  in the turning of the seasons,
    in the movement of the day,
      in the earth beneath our feet.
        And in silence.

Silence us, O God.
Lest our constant commentary drown out your quiet melody.
Lest our convincing arguments become attempts to shout others down.
Lest our noise be a way of denying
  the many places you are attempting to speak to us.
Silence us, and help us listen.
Silence us, and let us hear.
Help us remember
  that Jesus did not use organs, or hymnals,
  or suit and tie,
and yet through him,
  you were able to speak to us more clearly than anyone.
It is Jesus' pattern we follow now, as we pray together as he taught:
"Our Father, who art in heaven. . . ."

Free Us, God

I was looking through a song book the other day,
 and I came across a line of wisdom, printed at the bottom of the page.
It said,
  "Pay attention to the first thing you think about
  when you wake in the morning. It may be a clue to what you worship."

I must confess that the first thing I have thought about
  each morning for the last few weeks (besides going back to sleep),
  has been our house,
  and what still needs painting or patching before we sell it.
It is a recurring worry.

Think about what comes first to your mind most mornings—
  or what came first to your mind this morning.
If it was God, then you will have no trouble lifting your heart to God again
  in thanks and praise, in our moment of silence.
If it was not,
  then I encourage you to lift up to God what came first to your mind,
  with a prayer for release from obsession,
  and a prayer for freedom to live each day as a child of God.

In silence, we turn to our God.

[silence]

God who is beyond all, before all, above all, and in all,
  we turn over to you those things which grip our minds and hearts,
  and keep us out of your reach.

Please free us from the patterns of grief and guilt for things which have past:
  sins we have committed,
  sins committed against us,
  commitments neglected,
  losses,
  and the unending questioning, "What if I had . . . ?"

Forgive us. Restore us. Release us.

Please free us from our fears and anxieties over what lies ahead:
> what must be faced,
> what needs to be done,
> outcomes and results over which we have no control,
> and those which seem our sole responsibility,
> worry about work, and school, and family, and relationships.

Strengthen us. Renew our hope. Retell your promises.

Let our first thoughts be of you, O God.

Draw us like a magnet, always closer to you.

At our waking,
> may we rejoice and give thanks
> for the day you have made for us.

When we eat,
> help us to wonder at your gifts of scent and flavor,
> and the mysteries of our bodies' workings,
> and to give thanks for all you provide.

When we arrive at our work places,
> let us pray for your guidance and calm,
> to do our jobs as best we can,
> and leave the rest to you.

With our families,
> may we remember your love for us,
> so we may model it and share it with each one.

As we see the news,
> may we call on your compassion and justice,
> and offer ourselves as tools,
> for your kingdom in our world.

As we lie down to sleep,
    help us to give thanks for the day,
    to ask forgiveness for our shortcomings,
    and to turn ourselves over to your keeping,
    that we may rest peacefully.

Help us pray without ceasing.
Stand always before our faces.

Remind us that your loving kindness and mercy are new every morning.
For that you are greatly to be praised,
    again, and again, and again,
just as we have so often joined our voices to pray to you in this way:
    "Our Father, who art in heaven. . . ."

Goodbye and Look for Me

Today is a holy day on the church calendar. Ascension Sunday.
As holy days go, it's a minor one,
    although you would think that Jesus' departure from this earth,
    at least physically, would warrant more notice.
It is the Sunday before Pentecost,
    and it takes note of the six-verse story of Jesus
    promising to send the Holy Spirit to his disciples,
    and then rising into the clouds and disappearing.
I have usually not paid much attention to it,
    except as a signal of Pentecost's imminent arrival.
The story is a bit too supernatural and Spielberg-esque for my comfort.

But it has caught my attention this year.

I am intrigued by the way Jesus seems to say to his disciples
    in the same breath—"Good-bye," and "Look for me."

I am intrigued by the ending of Jesus' time on earth
    being so instant and anti-climactic.
        He evaporated.
        He was here then he wasn't—
    and yet, the disciples would tell you, he still was, still with them.

I am intrigued by the idea of looking for God's presence
    in what seems like God's absence.
Good-bye, and look for me.

In the silent prayer this morning,
    perhaps you can bring to mind a time, a place, a situation,
    which has felt absolutely empty of God.
And examine it
    for signs of God's presence.

[silence]

It was you, God, who in Christ assured us
  "I am with you always, even to the end of the age."
It was you who assured us
  that nothing could separate us from the love you have for us.

Why then, do we feel so abandoned so often?
Why does the world appear so out of control?
Where are you God?
We are looking for you, but there are days
  it feels as if you have simply said good-bye and left us.

When a teenager attempts suicide.
When yet another country falls into civil war.
When a beloved spouse is found to have brain cancer.
When a father dies.
When a chameleon of a virus makes AIDS run wild.
When the job held for twenty years vanishes.

We have called for you,
  and felt like we heard only the echoes of our own voices
  against empty walls.

If you are truly alive,
if you are truly the risen Christ,
if you are truly *with us*,
  let us know!

You promised.
You promised to fill us with power,
  to bathe us with the Holy Spirit,
  to send us comfort,
You promised to be with us.
Help us to find your presence,
  even if it is not in the expected, or hoped-for places,
  not in miraculous cures,
  not in spectacular deliverance,
  not in prayers granted like magic wishes.

Help us, like your first disciples, who had to stop looking for your person, Christ,
    and start feeling for your presence.
Help us, so we too may be filled with power,
        the power to do what must be done:
        to endure with strength,
        to restore with grace,
        to change directions with creativity,
        to reconcile with justice,
        and to love beyond sentimentality.

We will say good-bye to our preconceived ideas,
        and our worn smooth desires,
        if you will help us look for you, and *find* your presence
        in their absence.
May our hearts find you now,
        in and beyond the words our tongues can perform so well,
        as we join in this familiar prayer of Jesus, "Our Father, who art in
        heaven. . . ."

Fill Us with Power

Let us sing together, as we prepare ourselves to pray:

> *Spirit of the living God, fall afresh on me.*
> *Spirit of the living God, fall afresh on me.*
> *Melt me, mold me, fill me, use me.*
> *Spirit of the living God, fall afresh on me*
> (United Methodist Hymnal).

May we be open to the Spirit of the Living God,
> *as we await God's transforming touch, in silence.*

[silence]

O God of Pentecost's electrifying Spirit,
> we are all together in one place this morning.
We have held hands, we have prayed, and we have sung.
And we are waiting.

It seems we are often waiting
> for you to help us sort things out;
> for you to call us to action;
> for you steel our nerves and push us forward.

What is it those first disciples had that we don't?
Why did they feel the Spirit come with power, while we wait for even a tingle?

Come to us with power this day,
> and find some opening where you can slip into our lives.
Then fill us with power to overflowing,
> to the point where we must share you or explode.

Fill us, so that like the first disciples,
> we can shake off our fears, and step out of our sadness.
Fill us so we can stand up for you and take risks . . .

so we can risk speaking out
     though some will not understand;
so we can risk approaching someone different from us,
     though we don't know the right words;
so we can risk wearing our faith like a fiery red garment,
     though it makes us conspicuously different;
so we can risk giving away our precious time and money,
     though we don't know how it will be made up;
so we can risk letting go of what is past and outgrown,
     though the new is so frightening.

Help us risk, as individuals,
     as families,
     as a congregation,
     as the church of Jesus Christ around the globe.
Help us risk, not as blindfolded fools,
     but as those daring to walk in the faith,
     because we are filled with you,
     and charged with the Holy Spirit.
All of us who claim the name of Christ, near and far,
     are waiting.
And while we wait, we continue to pray the prayer that unites us as disciples.
"Our Father, who art in heaven. . . ."

Ordinary Time

God of Memory

Changes of seasons are, for me, times for opening doors in my memory.
    Maybe for you too.
It is as if the turn of the seasons turns over the soil,
        and unearths all the things which lay buried for the last year,
        bringing to the surface
            all the memories of all the summers that I have ever lived.
And they are all so tangible, it is as if they were happening right now.
Doesn't May bring you back to all the graduations you have ever been part of?
    All the gardens you have ever planted,
    all the vacations you have ever planned?
I think the turning seasons are one of the ways God has
        of keeping us in touch with our histories, personal, and communal.
And so, at the beginning of summer, on this Memorial Day weekend,
I invite you to use this silent prayer time in the holy act of remembrance.
Let us pray.

[silence]

Ancient God of memory, and of all that went before memory,
        our remembrance always turns us to you.
Why is it that each memory rediscovered is a surprise to us?
Did we not live through these things the first time?
Why is it that you have designed us so that all those feelings
        of joy and anticipation,
        or of terror and guilt,
        can present themselves to us as if new?

It is not that we are not grateful, God.
There are those people, those moments, those stories,
        whose memories quicken our pulse with delight.
In memory, our fathers are alive again,
        the applause after a concert still rings in our ears,
        and our ancestors come to this country, again and again.
Made in your image, we are given this capacity to make our past alive again.
        Thank you for this incomparable gift.
But there are times when the gift has its dark side, God.

Memory cannot be turned off.
    It bubbles like a spring, even when we try to suppress it.
And so in memory, we relive the terror of abuse,
        the anguish of leaving home,
        and the unrelenting grip of being at fault.
Sometimes, God, we would just as soon forget.

At those times, we remember that other gift you give: forgiveness.
It does not wipe the memories away,
        but it wipes away the tears.
It is only when the memories are crushing our spirits
        that forgiveness ceases to be an abstract idea,
        and becomes instead a welcome release.
Thank you God, for the gift of forgiveness,
        that allows us to carry the burden of memory.

Ancient God of all that has passed,
        we pray in remembrance of your son, Jesus,
        who taught us to pray saying: "Our Father, who art in heaven. . . ."

Shower Us with Gifts

Some days just feel like they are overflowing with celebration.
Despite what any headlines say,
>*or the pile of work to be done,*
>*or anything else,*

some days just seem to melt all that away, and leave only gleaming joy.
Today feels like one of those days.
I suppose it has to do with the celebration of an anniversary in ministry,
>*and a baptism for the second week in a row.*

It may have to do with a successful Vacation Bible School,
>*or a wedding yesterday.*

Or maybe it has to do with sunshine and irises, and my upcoming vacation.
I don't know which.
But it feels very right to praise and thank God this morning.
I invite you, in this time of silence,
>*to add your shining reasons for rejoicing to mine this morning,*
>*lifting up all the good you have seen in your life,*
>*or in the life of someone else in the community, and praising God.*

Let us pray.

[silence]

Let us pray to our God in whom we delight: Alleluia! Amen!

You, O God, are the reason for our joy.
You are the source of immense happiness and small pleasure.
You never stop looking for ways to give us, your children, happiness.
And so today, we pause to say, Alleluia! Amen!

You provide us, not only with daily bread,
>but with ice cream and cake as well.

We have not only enough to get by,
>but more, so our cups overflow.

Every time we turn around,
>we are met by your smiling presence in new and surprising garb.

For the ways you tickle us, we say, Alleluia! Amen!

It would be enough that you care for us,
    keep us safe, hear our prayers, meet our needs.
It would be enough for us.
    But not for you.
You do not rest, but shower us with gifts.
Sometimes you are more grandmother than father,
    more best friend than rock of security.
We can't get over it. So we shout Alleluia! Amen!

Our thankfulness is beyond measure.
    No gift we offer could ever repay you.
So instead, when we are filled to the brim by your goodness,
    let it pour out of us,
    drenching others with the joy you give us.
    And in the splash and spray, we will see you smile.
As we pray this, we hope that all our words and acts say Alleluia! Amen!
even as we join our voices to pray together the prayer which Jesus taught us,
saying, "Our Father, who art in heaven. . . ."

Gathered Prayer

Look around you.
No really.
This isn't a hypothetical request.
> *See who is sitting beside you, in front of you,*
> *behind you, across the aisle.*
These are the people who are here today that you are going to pray for—
> *and they are going to pray for you.*
In our silent time together, I want us to pray for each other.
> *By name if you like.*
> *You may wish to reach out and touch those nearby.*
> *Or you may just sit in silence,*
>> *and feel the strength of prayers offered up by many hands,*
>> *how light and easy that makes the work.*
In silence, pray for one another, and know that you are prayed for.

[silence]

In a chorus of silent voices, we have petitioned you just now, O God.
> We hope that you have heard.
We are not always in such harmony.
Oftentimes our voices of prayer clash with each other
> as we ask for things in such contradiction
> that you only, in your wisdom, could ever know how to answer them all.
And other times, our prayers are silent,
> leaving a few hoarse pleading throats
> to bear their burden of prayer alone.

God, just as it is easier to sing in a crowded sanctuary,
> so it is easier to pray in the midst of the joined wills
>> of the gathered congregation,
> where the strong voices can carry us over the difficult spots,
> and where the familiarity of another's wish
>> helps us to carry the tune with another.
God teach us to pray for each other.

You of a thousand ears,
we know that a prayer multiplied does not reach you better
by virtue of being louder.
Help us to feel the way that a prayer shared
is the beginning of a prayer answered,
and that you work your response to prayers
through the response of pray-ers.
When I pray for another, I crawl inside her skin,
and live with her for just that moment.
And in that moment, I can begin to see what can be, must be, done.

O God, from inside the skins of our neighbors, we lift up these prayers:
rejoicing in relief from pain;
yearning for a turn from addiction;
dragging the heavy weight of loneliness;
wondering at the newfound maturity of a child, nearly adult;
sighing for wasted years;
thrilling to a newly-discovered insight;
puzzling over the direction to take;
stretching beneath the burden of new responsibility.

God, knowing that some of these prayers are for ourselves,
and that those beside us pray them for us,
we begin already to feel you at work,
within our skins, within our souls.

It is with gratitude we turn to the way of praying which you taught us,
"Our Father, who art in heaven. . . ."

In Your Name

In the hymn we just sang, "Faith of our Fathers,"
    which words stay with you?
Do you remember, "dungeon, fire, and sword?"
    "true to thee till death?"
Or do you remember, "our hearts beat high with joy?"
    "we shall all be truly free?"
I ask that for a reason.
In our silent prayer this morning, I want to ask you to call on God.
I want you to use the eyes of your
    . . . imagination, yes, but not in the sense of making things up.
I want you to use the eyes of your heart, to look upon the face of God.

When you see the God to whom you have been praying lately,
    what expression does God wear?
Look closely as you pray.

[silence]

God, I wonder if we take you too seriously.

You remember the other morning,
    how beautiful it was, blue and green and clear,
    with the breeze coming through the kitchen window?
Do you remember how the breeze brought with it a scent as sweet as perfume?
Then you remember how I wrinkled my nose at first,
    reacting without thinking,
    that it was too sweet to be real, that it must be cheap cologne.

It was roses, God. Pink roses blooming by the sandbox.

I'm sorry for not recognizing it sooner.

Are we too grim to see you sometimes, God?
We resist the roses before we have even identified them,
    thinking they are too good to be true.

Why can't we relax and enjoy you?
Why can't we trust that you are good?

We are so sure of the grim agenda we suppose you to keep
      that we don't recognize your grace until it is almost too late.
We resist your call that says, "Wait! Stop!"
      until we have nearly sacrificed
            our children,
            our wives,
            our lives.
O God who made the first people to play in your backyard,
      don't let us miss the point.

When faith becomes so deadly serious it becomes deadly,
      keep us from killing one another in your name.
      Keep us from killing ourselves in your name.

When we make it harder to receive your grace as a gift
      than it was when we had to earn it,
          surprise us with roses,
          and put alternatives before our noses.

As we trudge along stooped over with our loads,
      sneak up behind us and lift them again,
      like you did when you sent Jesus to us,
      who tapped us on the shoulder and told us to
          leave behind those nets,
          and lay down those crosses,
          and follow him, empty-handed.

O God of Mercy,
help us to hear the joyful tune you have been humming all along,
      before it is too late.

With new eyes to see and new ears to hear,
we try again to pray as you taught your people to pray, saying, "Our Father, who
art in heaven. . . ."

Listen

Half of prayer is talking to God.
> *We don't think we are very good at it.*
> *We are not good with words.*
> *We are afraid we will get it wrong.*
> *We forget to do it.*
But it's a breeze compared to the other half: listening to God.
> *We know too many words.*
> *We are afraid what we might hear.*
> *We forget to do it.*

This morning, in the silence of the sanctuary,
> *try to clear a silent place in your minds as well.*
In silence, let us listen for God.

[silence]

Listen.
You bid us listen.
Those who have ears, let them hear.
We strain our ears for the sound of tiny seeds hitting the soil.
We are listening for you.
Sometimes we just miss it God.

> Pardon me? What did you say? I was watching TV.
> I was listening to my son whine.
> There was traffic outside my window.
> Were you talking to me?
Pardon me.
And teach us to tune out the noise
> that covers the muted pat of seeds hitting the earth.

Sometimes we misinterpret you God.
We think we have heard you, but we misunderstand.
> We think that your passion for justice means we should be judgmental.

We mistake your compassion for weakness.
We stone the sinner when we aim for the sin.
We listen to the cries of the world and wonder why you don't answer.
We are sorry God.
Teach us to hear the patter of seeds *in* the clatter of the world's activities,
    and to distinguish what you are really trying to say.
But sometimes, God, your seeds hit home.
Sometimes, all of a surprise, there is a moment
    when something we've heard all our lives sounds unfamiliar—
    as if we were hearing it for the first time,
    and as if it were meant for our ears only.
Sometimes—O glorious day—it all makes sense, it is clear.
A sentence in a sermon,
    the request of a child,
    the words to a song,
    an advertisement in a magazine—
suddenly turns the key,
and a door opens and the light of understanding pours in and it all makes sense.
And then we can't keep quiet.

Alleluia, thank you God of growth.
Teach us to echo the sounds of your seeds falling on the earth.

We listen even as we pray, as Jesus taught his followers: "Our Father, who art in heaven. . . ."

Drink Deeply

Breath of God, breathe on us,
          breathe *in* us,
     that we may breathe more easily.

God of unceasing love, we need to know your presence,
     for there are days when the world changes so fast,
     we cannot recognize it.
Sometimes it feels as if the world is on fire.
     Trouble rains down on us like sparks,
     and we turn and turn, trying to stem crisis after crisis.

Bills and illness, breakdowns and emergencies—
     we wish it would just slow down and let us deal
          with one at a time.
But the flames crackle on, and our lives are changed.
Around the world, nations smolder and burst into flame.
     Haiti. Rwanda. North Korea. Bosnia.
Sometimes we long for the old enemies,
     so at least we could recognize the landscape.
But the smoke of war blinds and chokes,
     and we stumble along in search of a landmark.

In the midst of the inferno, lead us to the still, cool reservoir
     that is your peace.
Bring us to the pool which cannot burn, and be our refuge.
Let us immerse ourselves in you,
     drink deeply of you,
     that we might face the fiery changes unafraid.

God of great stability,
     when our lives feel like quicksand,
     and all we thought secure becomes as gelatin beneath our feet—jobs,
          health, marriages, friends—
     when people whose love was a cornerstone of our lives

slip like sand between our fingers,
  moving, dying, growing away;
 Help us who are sinking, dig below the mire,
  and find there the bedrock that is *your* love.
All others may fall away. Your love will not be moved.

O God of all creation,
    as you show us again the shifting wonders of your universe,
    the shooting comet
    the day lily that blooms and fades by evening
    the dimpled elbow of a growing baby
    the mother-of-pearl sunset,
  cause us to gasp in awe,
  and discover again that you are
    as near as breath,
    as vital as oxygen,
    as present as air.

O God, our river, rock and wind, we thank and praise you
  for your unceasing, unchanging, unstoppable love.
In the name of Christ, your love incarnate, we pray. Amen.

Summer Prayers

This is summer, right? It's even starting to feel like it, finally.
This is the season where things lighten up, right?
The season to kick back and take it easy, catch our breath?
> *Then why are we so tired?*
> *Why are we so busy?*
> *Why do we have to work so hard at it?*

This is summer. And it's the Sabbath to boot, the day of rest.
So today, I'd like for us to be able to pray summer prayers.
So instead of suggesting a way for you to direct your silent prayers this morning,
> *I am giving you permission not to pray about anything in particular.*
> *Permission just to sit.*
> *And to listen.*
> *And to let things happen.*

For those of you who feel like you always have to be working on something,
> *think of this silent moment as a time to practice*
> *the discipline of letting go.*
In silence, let us rest in the presence of God.

[silence]

God, when we really let ourselves go,
when we really *let go*,
> being with you feels like coasting down a hill,
> like swaying in a hammock,
> like ice cream melting down our chin.
Your presence is that sweet.
Perhaps that is what heaven will be like—
> like relaxing into you, and ending our fevered racing.
Grant us, in these too-short months
> crammed with soccer balls, and vegetables to weed,
> with house paint and travel itineraries,
> permission to relax.

We need to taste the presence of heaven *now*.
In this green plateau of summer,
> we are closer than we will ever be at other times of the year-
> > times which cause us to brace, and flinch, and hurry.
For this is the lush season.
> The season of exuberant growth, and of sky-sized possibilities.
In *this* season, we might learn to trust.
> To trust that you will heal our wounds,
> and heal our world,
> and hold us tightly to your breast,
> and never let us go.
> To trust that you know what you are doing,
> > and that you want for us abundant joy.

God, this is the season of open hands,
> when you offer life so generously, extending open hands.
May it be the season we learn to relax *our* grip,
> open *our* hands,
> and let things slip in and out of *our* fingers,
> like sand and water at the beach.

We pray in the name of the one who knew when to work,
> and when to put the work aside,
> and who taught us how to trust in you, by praying, "Our Father, who
> art in heaven. . . ."

Forbidden

Jesus teaches us, when we pray,
> *not to be afraid or embarrassed, but to tell God what we need.*
I will admit, though,
> *that there are things it just doesn't seem appropriate to ask for:*
>> *winning the lottery,*
>> *my hair not turning gray,*
>> *a chance to sing on Broadway.*
It's not right to ask God to do these things for me.
> *But if it's not all right to admit them to God, then to whom?*
If we cannot share our dreams with God,
> *then with whom can we trust them?*

As we begin our prayers this morning,
> *I dare you to trust what Jesus says,*
> *and let God know what you wish for most,*
>> *even if it seems silly or selfish.*
Let us trust God with our prayers.

[silence]

God of all joy,
> we shyly open to you the hidden diary we keep.
Please don't laugh.
Please don't smirk at our selfish wishes for
> perfect wedding days,
> and children who are smarter than the others,
> and an evening when the phone doesn't ring.
Please don't laugh at the prayer we mumble
> as we begin a test,
> or bake a soufflé.
We know they are trivial matters in the grand scope.
> But they are joys of our desiring.

God of all hope,
> please do not sigh and shake your head when we pray for the impossible.
Do not shrug at our prayers for a life with no troubles,

for success in everything we do,
    for healing of even the incurable illness.
Don't look askance at us when the prayers which slip past our lips
    defy the laws of creation,
    and challenge the way you have made us.
Sometimes the longing for the impossible rises in us unbidden.
    Don't scold us for telling you about it.

God of all patience, don't be angry with our anger.
Don't condemn us when we pray
    that our team creams theirs,
    that we will beat the competition in the marketplace,
    that our enemies will have their faces ground in the dirt.
We have read in the Bible that the saints of old have prayed for worse.
Do not hold it against us when our bile spills over with curses in your name.

Jesus, joy of our desiring, you know what it is to be filled with human emotions.
    And so we risk revealing ours to you:
        our secret wishes;
        our unrealistic hopes;
        our uncensored anger.
Guide us in our prayers, and help us to reach deeper yet,
    and find beneath these requests
    the one which lies at the heart of all prayer—
We want to be well,
    to be at peace with each other and the world, and with you.
We want the serene confidence in the face of whatever we may meet
    that we know in you, Jesus.
We want to be like Christ.

Jesus, joy of our desiring,
    joy which we desire most,
    to you we pray.
Hear us as we pray,
    trusting in the way you have taught us to pray, saying, "Our Father, who
    art in heaven. . . ."

The Healing Touch

O God who holds body and soul together,
    though we often call upon you for healing,
    and count among our blessings, good health,
    we rarely stop to consider how great a thing we ask,
    and how many blessings work together
    in preserving our health.

We take for granted what works,
    and shrug off our little pains with a bit of complaint.
We pray in a broad way for miracle cures,
    and do not consider how miraculous all healing is.

This morning, we would pause,
    and feel out our bodies from within.
        We wiggle our toes and fingers inside our skin,
        We note the tensing and relaxing of muscles,
        We listen to the beating of our hearts,
        We focus on the drawing of each breath.
And as we do, we pray.
Those of us with limbs strong and limber enough
    to carry us where we wish to go,
    and to carry what we wish to bring along, give you thanks.
And those of us with joints that ache at every move,
    and legs and arms that tremble under their own weight,
    pray for your healing touch.

Those of us whose lungs fill easily and unconsciously with tingling air,
    give you thanks.
And those of us who labor for breath and struggle for oxygen,
    pray for your healing touch.

Those of us whose stomachs are often full,
    and whose appetites crave more of the good things you offer,
    give you thanks.

And those of us whose stomachs are corroded by hunger, or stress,
or who have no urge to eat,
pray for your healing touch.

Those of us whose minds are quick and clear and light,
give you thanks.
And those of us who are frightened by the gaps and slips,
or who are weighed down with depression,
pray for your healing touch.

Those of us who know that the systems
which intertwine in our bodies and give us life,
are in balance;
those of us who are eager to stretch and move and act,
give you thanks.
And those of us who must weigh carefully all that is eaten or done,
and whose thoughts turn constantly to what will ease the pain,
pray for your healing touch.

O God, maker of our every cell and tissue,
keeper of every nerve and muscle,
we thank you for how wondrously you have made us.

And knowing that you would love us to health,
each of us commends ourselves into your hands,
with both prayers of thanksgiving,
and prayers for healing.

Amen.

Many Gifts

"In our difference is blessing, from diversity we praise
one Giver, one Lord, one Spirit, one Lord"
(United Methodist Hymnal).

We like diversity . . . but mostly, we like to hang around with people a lot like us.
     We like people with whom we have something in common.
And so, because that is such an easy habit to fall into,
          I'd like us to take the opportunity this morning,
          to give thanks especially for those who are different from us.
In our silent prayer time, try to conjure up in your mind, a person you know—
          perhaps in this congregation—
          who is most unlike you.
Someone who takes part in different activities.
Someone who is good at different things.
Someone from a different kind of family,
          of a different age, or gender, or part of the world.
Someone with different politics or a different personality.

Perhaps it will be someone you dislike.
Perhaps it will be someone to whom you just don't usually pay much attention.
Whoever it is, look for the special gifts God has given to that person,
          and give thanks to God. Let us pray.

[silence]

God, at times I can only think of you as a grandma.
You always visit with a surprise in your purse.
          You never come empty-handed.
          You spoil us (but not really) with your gifts.
                    Door County cherries.
                    Meteor showers.
                    Cool nights after steamy days.
                    Children who grow into wonderful adults
                    stepping off on their own.
                    Music on the radio.
                    Music in the night sounds.

Conversations with neighbors.
But these gifts are nothing—just tokens—
    compared with the best gift of all from you,
    the first gift of all from you to us:
        Ourselves.
        And each other.
        Our lives.
        And our lives together.

We give thanks for each other,
    for the gifts they have received which complete our own,
    and enrich our lives.
For those who make music out of pieces of wood and brass.
For those who make poetry out of syllables and phrases.
For the consistency of those who never miss a Sunday.
For those who love our children enough to work with them.
For those whose passion for *doing* what needs to happen
    leaves us awestruck.
For those whose generosity with whatever they have
    leaves us wanting to give more ourselves.

For teachers who can make the complicated clear.
For craftspeople who can turn metal and wood into
    furniture and engines and homes.
For leaders who can get us to do things
    and enjoy it!
For followers, who can be counted on at any time,
    for any need.
For those who remember all about us,
    and always ask the right questions.

For children who throw themselves at our knees.
For young men and women who throw themselves into life
    with infectious enthusiasm.
For old women and men whose experience has taught them
    to know better than us, but who are patient nonetheless.
For those with a sense of humor and playfulness
    to keep us from taking ourselves too seriously.
For those who never let us forget what is really important.

What are we, God, *who* are we,
 that you have taken the time to fashion each one of us
 so differently and carefully and gloriously?
Who are we that you should give us each other
 to be a constant delight and help?
I guess we are your children.
Thank you.

We pray now with Jesus, our brother, who taught us when we pray to say, "Our Father, who art in heaven. . . ."

Hold Me, God

Lately, when I close my eyes to pray,
    I see somewhere just out of focus beyond thought,
    materializing somewhere above the words,
        an image.
It is an image I feel more than see,
    of God touching me skin to skin.
In it, I feel I am being held, cradled in God's arms like a small child—
    supported so that every muscle is relaxed,
    and my head is nestled in the crook of the neck beneath God's chin.

It has been a long time
    since I have been small enough to be snuggled this way by anybody.
Perhaps that is why the image is so persistent, and so beckons me—
    I long for the comfort it offers me.
I think that in these tired days of mine,
    above and beyond the words I pray,
    that image tells what I am really praying for.
In this time of silent prayer, I encourage you to turn off your mouths,
    including the mouths of your brain and their stream of silent words.
And look out beyond the dark at the inside of your eyelids,
    look with your skin and your muscles.
See if you can find the picture of what you are really praying for.
Be silent, and pray.

[silence]

God of wordless touch, sometimes when I pray,
    you pick up the beat of the music,
    and lead me by my fingertips to spin me,
    pirouetting around and around and around.
and I do not get dizzy, just carried away.
Sometimes in my prayers I sense you running beside me,
    racing me,
    until my chest aches for breath and excitement pounds through my veins.
And I feel as if I could execute an acrobat's string
    of flips and somersaults and cartwheels—effortlessly.

When I pray in the night,
	you come to me and tuck the cool sheets around my neck,
	brush the back of your hand on my cheek,
	and stroke my hair until I fall asleep.

There are times when I have prayed,
	and you have removed my hot, stiff shoes,
	and poured warm water over my bare toes.
I have pulled away in discomfort,
	both at the intimacy and tickle of your hands.
And sometimes as I finish praying,
	I feel your hand slip from mine.
But before I have the chance to react to the hollow in my palm and
	grasp for you,
	my hand closes on some small gift you have left there,
	smooth and dry,
	or furry and wriggling,
	and always a surprise.

But God, I notice when I pray,
	that I rarely stand with my arms outstretched toward you,
	facing you unprotected.
I think I am afraid that you will snatch me by the wrists
	and pull my arms from my sockets,
	and I will feel the rug burns on my knees
	as I am dragged away from comfortable prayers
	and out of the church into the glare of the sunlight.
When I pray, I know I risk you taking me where you want me to go.

God, we are thinking of holding our arms out to you.
I want to ask you to be gentle with us.
But you will do what you will do, O God of quiet firmness.
	So we pray that your will be done.

May our skin and muscles not flinch, but reflect our words,
as we pray together in the way in which Jesus taught us:
"Our Father, who art in heaven. . . ."

Change

This week I was struck
> *by several abrupt and startling changes in the world around me:*

On Wednesday,
> *ten houses on the next block were torn down,*
> *making a level plain out of a neighborhood*
> > *that had for over eighty years been homes.*

On Thursday, we awoke to find that summer had fled overnight.
> *Temperatures had dropped nearly thirty degrees;*
> *shorts gave way to jackets, and it was abruptly autumn.*

And on Friday, a new window was installed in a room in our house,
> *flooding it with light, and opening new views to our yard.*

Change occurs with suddenness that leaves us speechless—
> *but I hope, not without a prayer.*

This morning, let us pray for people who have turned a blind corner
> *in their lives,*
> *and find the world will never be the same.*

Let us lift our hearts to God in prayer.

[silence]

O God, in the midst of the new rubble, the new chill, and the new brightness
> that interrupts our lives and the lives of others,

we turn to you,
> our foundation, fiery spirit, and light of lights.

And we pray for your constancy and comfort
> to calm those for whom change comes as an attack:
> when a diagnosis of cancer suddenly fills the future
> > with chemotherapy and uncertainty;
> when a miscarriage erases from the future
> > a due date and a child;
> when a mother's death amputates the past
> > and leaves one orphaned;
> when an accident takes loved ones without warning,
> > and leaves hearts bleeding.

For these, we pray, that you, O God, will be there, as rock and redeemer.

We pray for your energy and hope to gush through those
        for whom change comes as a surprise party:
        when adoption drops a baby into a family
                so fast there isn't time to prepare;
        when surgery alleviates a pain
                that had threatened to last beyond endurance;
        when reconciliation with one loved and lost,
                dawns after a night of estrangement;
        and when your presence is suddenly recognized and received
                as a gift that has been hidden in plain sight.
For these, we pray that you will be transfigured—
        new, and yet delightfully familiar.

We pray today as well, for those for whom change is ambiguous,
        and comes as a fog bank:
        when a new job changes the route commuted,
                and the tasks of eight hours a day;
        when awakening in a new home brings consciousness
                of unfamiliar promise and unfamiliar responsibility;
        when a new semester in a new school makes one feel
                so grown up, and so young at the same time;
        when a child leaving for college makes one feel
                so fulfilled and so empty at the same time;
For these, we pray that you will bring clarity and direction,
        and be a light unto their path.

"God of change and glory,
        God of time and space,
When we fear the future,
        give to us your grace.
In the midst of changing ways,
        give us still the grace to praise" (United Methodist Hymnal).

We pray in the name of Jesus Christ
        whose resurrection changes forever,
        not only his life,
        but each of ours,
and who taught us to pray in this way:
"Our Father, who art in heaven. . . ."

The Power of Love

Lord Jesus Christ,
    Dinner companion of sinners,
    Party host to the unlovable,
    Defender of prostitutes,
    Befriender of the scum of the earth,
forgive us for acting as if sin is contagious,
    and we are disease free.

We confess that we are prone to act
    as if the church were a sterile compound
    that only the healthy may enter.
We are proud of our righteous lifestyles,
    we are pleased we have made the right choices
    with our lives, our actions, our resources.
And we choose to surround ourselves
    with those who live as we do—
    healthy lives,
    away from the germs of sin:
        poverty,
        alcohol,
        promiscuousness,
        gambling,
        foul language,
        violence.

Forgive us for acting as if sinners should be quarantined,
    and the self-righteous should be free
    to spread our disease.

We confess that we deny the truth about sin,
    and how it comes to infect us.
We don't recognize the symptoms,
    or see the telltale signs,
    in our own faces.

We pretend we can be immune,
　　　　that we can vaccinate our children against sin,
　　　　if only we can avoid contact
　　　　　　　with those people,
　　　　　　　those sinners.
We do not want to accept
　　　　that sin is not caught from the outside,
　　　　but grows from within like a cancer.

O great physician, who came not to those who are well,
　　　　but to those who are ill,
　　　　show us again what is truly contagious.
Jesus, great lover of our souls,
　　　　catch each one here by the hands,
　　　　in tenderness, let us drink from your cup,
　　　　hold us in your embrace and kiss us on the mouth,
　　　　for the most virulent virus of all, is your love.
Once we have caught your love, we can never be cured.
Once we are infected with your love,
　　　　we become carriers,
　　　　passing on to all with whom we come into contact
　　　　　　　this great love,
　　　　　　　the stronger virus,
　　　　that drives out our sin,
　　　　and leaves us with the antibodies to sin
　　　　to allow us to befriend sinners
　　　　　　　as you did,
　　　　　　　without fear.

You who taught us that perfect love casts out fear,
You who showed us that perfect love is stronger than sin and death,
　　　　send us out in the power of that love,
　　　　until it is epidemic in our world.

Great healer,
　　　　may we *serve* as you have taught us,
　　　　as faithfully as we *pray* as you have taught us,
　　　　saying, "Our Father, who art in heaven. . . ."

For Teachers

Today we honor our Sunday School teachers.
We have listed them for you.
Look at the list of teachers, and choose one to pray for by name.
> *It may be the teacher of one of your children's classes.*
> *It may be your teaching partner.*
> *It may be the teacher of the class you will attend.*
> *It may be the teacher of the class you taught before.*
> *It may be the one you know is new.*
Whoever you choose, in our time of silent prayer,
> *hold that person before God,*
> *and pray for the ministry*
> *they have among the people of God.*
In silence, we pray.

[silence]

Jesus, our teacher,
> you once held a child in the midst of your followers,
> and told them that to welcome the children
> was to find themselves in the very presence of God.

We pray for the children you have put in the midst of this congregation.
Most of them are not in this room with us,
> but we can feel their presence.
Just past these walls, the rooms are full of them.
May the time they spend in those rooms, and among us, shape them.
May they know your love for them.
May they grow into disciples who serve in your name.

We pray for those who welcome the children on our behalf—
> the Sunday School teachers who greet them
> > with smiles and stories and Scotch tape.

Fill those teachers with love for your story, Jesus,
    so that their enthusiasm will rub off on those who learn,
    and leave them shining.
We pray for those who welcomed us, when we were only children.
Their faces and voices line our memories.
    In them, you came to life for us.
Thank you for those who have taught us.

We pray for ourselves, this day.
Surprise us with new understandings of old stories.
Make fresh for us the faith that was planted in us long ago.
Nudge and tickle us,
    so that we are never satisfied with what little we know of you,
    but are challenged to keep searching for your truth
    until we know you face to face.

Lord Jesus, in welcoming the children, may we indeed greet you as well.

We pray now, following the pattern learned at your feet,
saying together, "Our Father, who art in heaven. . . ."

I Am Thine

"I am thine, O Lord."
    I am whose?
Belonging to someone is not an image which strikes a chord with us.
    As a matter of fact, it doesn't sit well at all with us.
    It smacks of slavery and indentured servitude.

We don't even give brides away any more—
    a woman isn't the property of her father or her husband.
We are a nation of tough individuals, who idealize independence.
And yet . . .
    we sing, "I am thine, O Lord."

In our time of silence together,
    I invite you to pray that phrase, and nothing more.
    "I am thine, O Lord."
And feel what it does to how you look at your life.
In silence, we pray.

[silence]

God, I'm nobody's woman but my own.
Nobody tells me what to do. I am in charge of my life.
    I think.
But God, sometimes I wonder, sometimes I think we all wonder . . .
    are we really our own people?

I don't know how many times a day I hear people say to me,
    "I would if I had the time. I'd do that for the church.
    But my job is so hectic. My family keeps me hopping.
    I'd really like to . . . but I can't."
I believe they do really want to, God.
Just like I believe them when they roll their eyes and sigh about their work.

Lots of people don't like what they do all day, God.
    But they can't quit.

And a lot of people like what they do,
  but don't want to do so much of it.
But work dictates our schedules,
  and shapes our daily lives,
    and sets our priorities.
Do we belong to our jobs?

When it seems to be so, we pray, "I am thine, O Lord."

I see a lot of people with a lot of stuff, God.
  Things.
Things that take a lot of time and money.
  Cars. Boats. Houses. Stereos—Me, too.
We paint them and polish them, and wash and clean them.
  We fill them and remodel them and replace them and accessorize them.
I wonder sometimes, do we possess our things, or do they possess us?
Possession.

When we think we are possessed, we pray . . .
"I am thine, O Lord."

I am thine . . .
  I belong to you like a husband to a wife—
  we are bound to each other in love.
I am thine . . .
  I am your child. I am held in your embrace.
  I am secure in my trust of you.
I am thine . . .
  I belong to you like a bird belongs to the air—
  it is in you that I am most at home,
  and most free to do what I am meant to do.
I am thine . . .
  I am marked by your sign in the water of baptism,
  I am called by your name—Christian. By you I am known.
I am thine, O Lord.
May it never be otherwise.

And now, we who belong to each other in you,
  join our voices to pray as you have taught us in Jesus,
  saying, "Our Father, who art in heaven. . . ."

Come In

Through Jeremiah, God said,
"The days are coming . . . when I will put my law within them,
and I will write it on their hearts,
and I will be their God and they shall be my people."
Let us examine our hearts, and look for God's handwriting there.

[silence]

God, as the nights encroach on the days,
and the chill fingers of winter reach down into our coat collars,
we are increasingly conscious of the line
between in and out,
and we shut the door more firmly behind us every day.

Forgive us that we slam the doors of our hearts
and leave you shivering outside.
Forgive us our busyness and hurry,
that give you no opportunity
to speak with us, call us, challenge us.
Forgive us our greed to have all, do all, be all,
that fills our hearts to capacity
and leaves us to shrug our shoulders at you.
Forgive our despair at the state of our world,
that prevents us from trusting you
to begin to make a difference,
and will not open our hearts
no matter how loudly or often you knock.

Forgive us the rigidity of our loving,
which feels that we have loved to the limit,
and will not stretch our hearts
to admit those you send to us.

God, you have promised to write your promises in our hearts,
and you can only do that from within.
We pray that you will find a way we have not blocked.

Come to us through the windows of our weakness.
Slip in through the gaps our doubts have opened.
Break into our dreams when we are sleeping.
Rush us when we are off guard.
Come in unfamiliar guise, so we will open the door a crack.

Come to us, God,
    and open the door from within,
    so you may take up residence in our hearts,
    and from that dwelling place
    fill the world with your light and warmth.
O God, like clouds of breath on an autumn day,
    our prayers rise to you.
Come, and make our hearts your home.

We join now, heart with heart and voice with voice,
    praying as we have been taught to pray: "Our Father, who art in
    heaven. . . ."

Mark a Path

"Where Charity and love prevail, there God is ever found."

Or, more simply translated,
Where love is, there is God.

A great deal of Christian theology can be boiled down
to that essence of who God is.

Where love is, there is God.

This morning, think about where you saw love,
felt love,
experienced love in action this week.
And in our moments of silence together,
say, "Thanks God—it was good to see you."

[silence]

Our God, who is never far from us,
lean near to us and hear our prayer this morning.
Forgive us, ever-present God, for putting you too far from us.
For looking only into the clouds of heaven
and at the beginning and end of this life.
For attributing to you
only the high profile miracles
and the oracles of the distant past.
For reserving you on a shelf under glass
for a rainy day,
or in case of emergency.
Forgive us for keeping you away—
or rather, for not recognizing your nearness.
For in reality, nothing can keep you from us.
And wherever we know love,
there you are.
Thank you for being here.
Thank you for having been in our week.
In the everyday kindnesses

of doors held, and please and thank you.
In the dishwasher unloaded without a request.
In the phone call in the middle of the day.
In the kiss goodnight.
In hand-me-down shoes.
In temperatures taken,
and tickles given.
In visits as reliable as clockwork.

We are used to looking for you, for *seeing* you
in baby blankets,
and wedding vows,
and funeral embraces.
And we are glad you are there.

But in between, it's easy to take you for granted.
So today, we remember that in every act of love,
there you are.
And we take delight in the recognition,
saying, "Oh! It was you!"

The next time we hear someone cry out for you, God,
The next time we wish you would come
and end some mess, God,
The next time we see someone sigh in loneliness for you—
we will remember
that where love is, there you are.

And we will begin loving
to mark a path for you
to announce your coming
to be your warm hands
and the breath of your presence.
For whenever we love, you are with us.

Because this is true,
we look to the one who is love made flesh for us, Jesus Christ,
and we pray as we were taught, saying . . .
"Our Father, who art in heaven. . . ."

Promises

In case you had forgotten, or hadn't noticed yet, this is pledge Sunday.
It's the day we offer to God our promises
    for how we will serve God in the coming year—
    with our financial resources,
      but I hope as well, with all of our resources:
        time, and talent, and effort.

With those promises in mind, let us turn to God in prayer.

[silence]

God, you are both generous and jealous,
    and your hands hold out for us
    both requirements and redemption.

And so, in thanksgiving, we turn to you,
    and out of responsibility, we make promises.
We pray today for the promises we make
    to each other,
    and through those promises, to you.

We pray for all who have made promises,
    that you will strengthen them to keep them.
For those who make vows to love, honor and cherish a spouse—
    whether this weekend, or fifty years ago;
    may their promises feed their love each day,
    and carry them through the days when love seems weak.
We pray for those who take oaths to serve as our leaders—
    Judges, presidents, council chairpersons,
    police officers, and pastors;
May their promises keep them honest, and fearless,
    and direct the decisions they must make.
We pray for those who consecrate themselves for your work—
    Susan as she leaves for Africa this week,

Richard and Caring, who serve as missionaries
in the storm-struck Philippines,
the Sunday School teachers who spread your word
each week, just down the hall.
We pray also, for the promises we make this day, and each day,
either aloud, or in our hearts.
Take our hopes for those who are ill,
turn them into phone calls and visits and casseroles,
so that they know your loving touch.
Take our intentions to serve the poor,
and schedule them for a Tuesday at the homeless shelter,
fill them with canned goods for the care baskets,
and impose them as limits
on our own extravagant living.
Take the feelings of our hearts toward our loved ones,
and temper our loud voices when angry,
nerve our challenges to their unwise choices,
and open our calendars to time with them.
We pray especially for the promises we make to you this hour:
Give us courage to follow through on our pledges,
even when it feels risky to give so much.
Excite us to new giving, by showing us
how even small gifts have huge results in your hands;
And don't let our fears of serving you imperfectly,
keep us from serving you at all.

O God, source of all promise,
and keeper of the greatest promise of all,
we pray to you in the name of the Christ,
who gave us this pattern for praying:
"Our Father, who art in heaven. . . ."

Answer Us!

There are many times we pray, and we are not sure we are heard.
As we pray this morning,
>   *I offer you again the words*
>   *which were read to us from Hebrews a few moments ago:*
"Let us hold fast to the confession of our hope without wavering,
>   *for he who has promised is faithful."*

Let us pray.

[silence]

God, we bow before you on Sunday mornings, and call to you.
We pause a moment before our meals, and call to you.
We turn our last thoughts to you before we sleep, and call to you.
We stand by the bed of a loved one who is ill, and we call to you.
We watch the evening news, and we call to you.
We confess God, that as often as we call to you,
>   we sometimes fail to expect any response.
We turn to you as much out of habit as hope.
We pray as much because we have despair, as because we have faith.
>   Who else can we turn to?

We admit that sometimes, all we want to do in prayer is yell at you.
>   Heal him! He's a good man! He doesn't deserve this!
>   Save those children!
>   How could you let a mother do such a thing?
>   Bring them back! That accident was so senseless!
>   Lift her burden! She's suffered long enough.
>   Stop the violence! Too many have been hurt there!

Do you hear us?
Are you listening?
Why don't you *do something*!
>   You are God. Do something.

God of boundless patience, we do not have your ability to wait.

We do not understand delays.
Some days, we cannot fathom what you are doing in the world.
Today, as we bow before you and call to you,
    answer us.
If you cannot give us exactly what we ask,
    at least let us know that you have heard us ask.
Remember us, hear our distress,
    and fill us with the love that encourages endurance,
    and the hope that produces patience.
The world came from your hands, and into your hands we place it.
    Care for your creation, and us as a part of it.

And as we wait, may we have the confidence of your children,
    who everywhere join their voices to say,
    "Our Father, who art in heaven. . . ."

The Provider

"All I have needed thy hand hath provided."

This is a truth about our God that we sometimes neglect.
It is hard some days to come up with an example
         of a blessing we have received.
Everything we have,
         seems to have come from our own sweat and toil.

And yet, each day, we are blessed dozens of times.

If we were to examine our days, by asking ourselves,
         "What did I need to live out this day?"
         we might learn to tune ourselves to all that God does for us.

And so I challenge you to do that this morning in our silent prayer.
Choose a day from this week, and examine it,
         asking, "What did I need to live out that day?"
You may find you have more for which to be thankful than you realized.

May we join now in silence before God.

[silence]

We pray to you, O Faithful One,
         with something of gratitude,
         and something of embarrassment,
         and something of awe.

We come before you to say thank you for the ways our needs are met each day:
         When our stomachs growl, there is food to fill them—
         Food in great plenty, overfilling our cupboards,
         going forgotten and spoiling in our refrigerators.
         Food in great variety,
                  crunchy carrots, toasted bread,
                  sticky oranges, and steaming cocoa.
We are blessed.

When the weather turns cold, we have ways to stay warm:
    A roof on which the rain can patter,
    A door to close against the wind.
    A coat with deep pockets and heavy lining,
    Turtlenecks to stop the draft.
We are blessed.

When our bodies and minds are weary, we have renewal.
    We have deep dreamless sleep.
    We have hugs from our parents.
    We have letters from a great distance,
        and laughter on the phone.
We are blessed.

Every day, we are blessed.
All I have needed thy hand hath provided.

And so it is with some embarrassment we come into your presence.
For some of us, it has been awhile since we noticed these everyday blessings,
    and a longer while since we expressed our gratitude.
With such constant blessings,
    one would think we would feel rich and generous.
But instead we dwell a great deal on what we do not have,
    and very little on what we do.
It is a hazard of our society.
But we are sorry for having fallen prey to it.
Gracious one, you hear our confession and offer forgiveness.
Again, you have provided for our needs, and we are blessed.

It is also with some awe that we come before you.
For we have known you to answer prayers
    we were afraid to utter.
We have known you to bless us beyond our deserving.
We have known you to provide for hungers we had not known we felt
    until they were satisfied.
And we have known the wonder,
    the absolute awe,
    of stepping out past where our security lies,
    of jumping into the abyss of risk,

of reaching into a dark uncertainty,
and finding ourselves borne up
by the wings of your faithfulness.
For we find that our stores are not emptied,
but our cup overflows.
We are blessed. Each day we are blessed.
And so we pray with strength and confidence,
the prayer claimed by all who trust in your faithfulness, saying,
"Our Father, who art in heaven. . . ."

For Life, for New Life

November is the month of the graying of the year,
    the season of the shutting down of the light.

On this last Sunday of the church year,
        when things grind to a halt before the frenzy of the holidays,
        let us pray for new life.
                New life for ourselves.
                New life for those we love.
                New life for those we have never met,
                        but whose spiritual or physical dying is known to us.
                New life for the church, and all of us who compose it.
In silence, we pray for new life,
        as different from the old as snow is from sleet,
        as the butterfly is from the chrysalis.
In silence, will you pray with me . . .

[silence]

God of resurrection, in a season that looks like death,
        we dare to pray for new life,
        because we can smell the hope on your breath.

For those of us who walk back and forth
        between the two poles of work and home,
        in an ever-shortening route that threatens to close in on itself
                and leave us tethered to a pin,
                marking time,
                unable to get anywhere,
                or reach beyond ourselves—

That there is more to life than this, we pray.
We pray for life, for new life.

For those of us whose lives are lived
        in the shadow of the threat of death,
        for whom that stain of darkness obscures the future,

cutting it so abrupt and near
         that there is no room even in the present—
That there may be life after death, and life before it, we pray.
We pray for life, for new life.

For those of us embarking on the journey
         from the fresh and unworn end,
             at whose side our partners are yet unfamiliar and untested,
             whose course is only sketchily drawn,
             whose destination is but a hazy figment—
That we may travel unencumbered, and unafraid, we pray.
We pray for life, for new life.

Whenever we pray, we pray in the name and spirit of the Christ,
         the giver of life and of new life.
We pray together in the way of his disciples, saying,
         "Our Father, who art in heaven. . . ."

Before the Feast

Come Thursday evening,
you're gonna find it hard to believe you'll ever be hungry again.
But right now,
before the feast,
I invite you to take some time
to ponder the places and ways you are empty.
What is it you hunger for?
What is it you crave?
In our silent time this evening,
take to God your prayers for those parts of you
which growl to be filled.

[silence]

God, you satisfy the hungry heart.
We lift up to you the hollows and voids we feel.
A lack of food or the money to buy it.
A longing for security.
A yearning for a love we can trust.
An ache for a piece of our lives lost,
that stings like a wound that won't heal.
A sigh for an opportunity gone.
The need to belong somewhere, to someone.
A craving to know *you,* God.
We tell you of this hunger, God, and pray to be filled.

We know we can pray to you,
because we trust that you satisfy the hungry heart.

We have known emptiness before,
and now know the contrast of hearts brimming with blessings.
We have found that our needs have been met,
not just to satisfaction,
but you have filled us with delicacies.
The empty tomb of mourning has been filled,
not just with passing time,

but with peace and comfort.

The echo of loneliness has been muffled,
    not just with busyness,
    but with love and acceptance.

The yawning cavern of fear and uncertainty has been bridged,
    not just by distraction,
    but by confidence that you are near.

The hollow purposelessness of our lives have been crammed full,
    not just with things,
    but with passion for you, and for your ways, O God.

And so we approach you with gratitude,
       immense gratitude,
    for all that we have, and all that we are,
    for everything from the air we breathe to sustain our bodies,
    to the love we breathe to sustain our souls.

And we say thank you, God,
    for satisfying our hungry hearts.

Fill us again, from your stores which are never depleted.

And now, as those who know the good gift of Christ,
    and live as followers of Christ,
    we pray together as we were taught by Christ:
    "Our Father, who art in heaven. . . ."

Afterword

THERE IS AN OLD SAYING "GREAT OAKS FROM LITTLE ACORNS grow." However, acorns must have the proper climate, atmosphere, and nurturing to grow.

So it is with many other things in nature. Unless flowers are watered, fertilized, and served with sunshine, they cannot share their beauty with others.

The weekly prayers of the Reverend Karen Ebert create beautiful and inspirational images of God for her congregation. But unless they are given permanence in printed form, only a small number of people can benefit.

We believe that Pastor Ebert's prayers are so unique, create so many personal visions and have such reflective imaging power, that they should be shared by everyone. And thus, this inspirational prayer book.

P. J. H. /E. B. H.

About the Author

KAREN EBERT received a B.A. in psychology from the University of Wisconsin–Madison, and a M.Div. from Garrett-Evangelical Theological Seminary, Evanston, Illinois. She is an ordained minister of the United Methodist Church and is currently associate minister at First UMC, Green Bay, Wisconsin. Ebert previously served at St. Paul's UMC in Stevens Point, Wisconsin. She and her husband, Wes, have two children and reside in Green Bay.